Runes From The Rhine

Silent City
and
Other Poems

by

Louis R. Fendrick

illustrated by

Anne R. Knight

Windswept Press
Interlaken, New York
1988

Manufactured in the United States of America
ISBN: 1–55787–032–2

A *qualtity* publication by
Heart of the Lakes Publishing
Interlaken, New York

RUNES

Just another word for poems

THE RHINE

A poorer section of the canal town
Ithaca, New York. A segment of the Erie
Canal. The Rhine, sometimes known as
Shanty Town or Silent City.

To my granddaughter

Jennifer Ann

SILENT CITY

Within the framework of any city
lay the slums, where more the pity
unfortunates in life, drift in space
to a haven they will call their place.

Now in our town where I grew up,
there was just such an area corrupt
across the tracks we called the Rhine
to a place where sun did not shine.

Along the Inlet a swampy section
became for folk an urban infection.
Among cat-tails they made on stilts
the shanty shacks, all jerry built.

Joined by catwalks, slim and narrow
one to another and as such they grew
to form their Utopia, their ideality
we came to know as Silent City.

A place for bums, drifters of sorts,
a refuge for the evaders of courts.
We were told even the cops did not dare
to go in alone, and not have a care.

Now a city within a city, cannot be,
and people should not live for free.
The city we knew as Silent, once more
caused the populace to even the score.

So it came to pass, as all could see
the local committee could not agree
to this marriage, not made in Heaven
so city fathers torched it in 1927.

Silent City was no more!

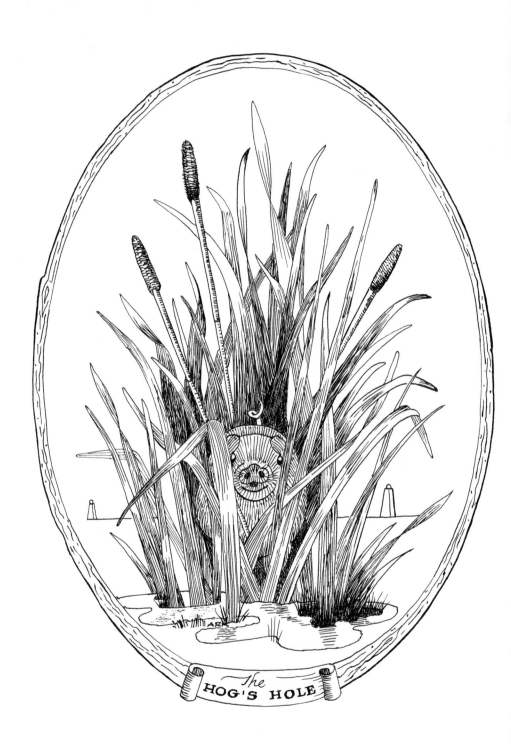

The
HOG'S HOLE

"THE HOG'S HOLE"

Beyond the cat-tails awash from the lake
cradled in the bend, Lighthouse to shore,
there is the area, one cannot mistake
and really one that we cannot ignore.

Spawning grounds for North' pike and eel,
the wintering spot for ducks and geese.
The poacher's haven with greater appeal
for a bounty untold and never to cease.

Off the lake and into this Bog's Shoal
squatters come and some would go.
It came to be known as the "Hog's Hole"
or as the early settlers called it so.

Where the name came from in the past,
none of us has really known it to be,
but tales do tell us of one outcast
deep in the swamp with name of "Hoggy."

Others claim a farmer with a wagon loaded
with a boar hog, tipped over in the mire,
mud and muck of the old Glenwood Road.
The hog escaped into the swamp inspired.

The hog was searched for but never found,
or so the early legend has it been said.
There are others say it was taken aground,
killed, and of how the squatters were fed.

And so it has been told in verse and song
and of how the hog played the slog role,
but all in all, you see, we could be wrong,
as to how it's been called the "HOG'S HOLE."

"BALLAD OF BOGIE"

On the outskirts of our fair city
   and in the swamps along the Inlet
     lived the hero of this witty ditty,
      a tough guy, and one you won't forget.

Some say his true name was Bodie,
   but by and large along the barge
     he acquired this name of Bogie,
      and of this we will not enlarge.

Quick of wit and of an Indian birth
   he was a scrounger down in The Rhine.
     With a glowering look and never mirth,
      he was truely one of a kind, any kind.

Badgering for drinks down at the GLOBE
   Bogie made the unforgiveable mistake.
     Not too sharp, not wisely did he probe
      into affairs of toughs from the lake.

Strong hands lifted Bogie high above,
   over the heads of the men at the bar.
     Through swinging doors they did shove
      and threw our Bogie way out and afar.

He landed with a splash, and I think
   bubbly he noisily sank beneath the water
     in a concrete trough where horses drink
      and our Bogie really hadn't oughter.

It seems one thing led to another
   as Bogie's luck was not too bold.
     Word got out one way or the other
      the Feds were after him we're told.

He headed for the swamps, a step ahead
of the cops with charges of old, untold.
   The end of catwalks stopped him dead
      so he jumped into the water icy cold.

He swam the Inlet urged by the fear
leaving his pursuers by the shack.
   He made it to the Lighthouse Pier,
      once ashore, he never looked back.

Legend has it that he evaded arrest
but tells us of his acquired cold,
   illness that would not let him rest,
      a year more or so we have been told.

All his escapades could fill a book
of barges, trains, and of bridges too,
   but of the man with the glowering look,
      we can only render this Ballad true.

RETICENCE

Wearily, aware I greet each day
   not knowing really what to say.
Verily, aware, I meet the sun
   not really knowing who has won.

SQUIRREL

Chattering, chatting, nervous fluff of gray
    scolds me at my close approach.
Sensing, scenting, he puts his bluff away
    and eyes my bold encroach.
Scary, yet wary, behind a bough he hides
    and flicks his brush at my every step.
Scurry and hurry, atop the tree he glides
    to fade away into the den he kept.

SPRING

Rain melts the snow, and the geese fly high.
    Willows now begin to show buds out to the sky.
Streams are filled with a sudden surge,
    and fish return with their spawning urge.

The days now grow on with longing light,
    and Robins arrive in their awesome flight.
It's getting to be that time again,
    the snow has gone, peepers in song begin.

FARMER'S MARKET WOES

Down at the West End on the Boulevard,
    now the dead-end of the railroad yard.
Designated local site Farmers' Market.
    Resignated focal sight where to park it.

Location of that land is now contested
    as merchants at hand deplore congestion.
With one road of entry, space allowed,
    plea to relocate gentry is voiced aloud.

Solution was seen to check ebb and flow.
    Lights red and green move cars to and fro.
But problems abound and with it dissension.
    No answer is found so further apprehension.

Could we only but share, root of our labor
    without knowingly aware of brute neighbor.
We are not without fault, neither are you,
    so come to a halt, or we must never do.

Each go to City Fathers to seek a relief,
    as Committee bothers in an oblique belief.
One for the Farmers, and two for the show,
    three for the Enders, another place to go.

A TRIBUTE TO HENRY

Henry and I.
We grew up on the North Side,
a walking distance to our school.
A sliding walk from here to there,
with winter snow slickening the way.

Those city blocks we had to cover
included one we could not avoid.
And pugnacious Jimmy waited for us
with a desire to "Make his day."

We survived and attended High School
me busy with my paper route,
and Henry with his heart in sports.
In time to become a four letter man.

Then came the War, Number II that was.
Me in the Navy, he in the Air Force.
Somehow we made it back to our town
and years later our paths would cross.

Kismet, so it came to pass, we met
having our breakfast at McDONALDS.
We relived our past with fond recall
joined by John, Joe, Billy, others too.

We missed him one day and I got a call
from John, his buddy, closest of all.
"He's gone Lou, I found him there at home
with Muggsy, his cat by his chair."

Henry Johnson had died.

HOMETOWN

Sheltered by those shaded hills.
Guarded by sky blue waters,
lies a land of lakes and rills
with her sons and daughters.

Deeply set within her heart
is the town I love.
A royal jewel set apart
by the great One above.

Restful haven for friendly folk
who this way would venture,
to free a burden, to rest the yoke
of travel and adventure.

FRIENDSHIP

A true friend is hard to find,
and twice as hard to lose.
A real friend doesn't mind,
the kind of life you choose.
Your griefs and joys he will share,
at your side when the going is tough.

With a happy smile and not a care,
he doesn't mind it being rough.
To have one is to be one,
for they are never found
When your battles are done,
but when all troubles abound.

SABELLA

There is a story that has been going around
    about a character in our town, long ago.
    Sabella was her name I want you to know,
    who fancied her voice an operatic sound.

We recall her debut in our college town
    and her solo concerts in our local hall
    prompted by eager students, one and all
    urging her to perform in a voice renown.

Her hand-lettered posters became a sight
    around our town and at the movie show
    inviting all folk with a colorful glow
    to enjoy together an operatic night.

Tickets in hand we waited in line
    and as doors opened we rushed to our seats
    in manner of youth, not too discreet,
    we noisely awaited with ultra design.

As curtains parted she took the stage
    and with opened arms embraced us all
    as hoots and hollers filled the hall
    from provoked students coming of age.

Her bosom bedecked with a red, red rose
    and legs stockinged in pink or blue
    her gown of print in contrasting hue
    prepared Sabella for her evening show.

Music came from the piano way below,
    and her first high note split the air
    as her off-pitch chord raised one's hair.
    Sabella had started her show, as we know.

Shrieks of laughter bounced off ceiling
    joined by vocal "I Love You Truly" and
    the feigned applause became so unruly, yet
    she continued to sing lost in her feeling

One really can't say, she had no flair
    for entertaining with her song antics
    because she dared with some romantics
    to sing, she said, because she cared.

Concert over, she signed autographs
    and for her fans, she threw out the rose.
    Her reason why, no one really knows,
    but even so, we joined in the laughs.

They say I have "Bees in my bonnet" yet
    they pay for tickets to hear me sing.
    So, am I the fool, the crazy old thing,
    or am I the heroine of this sonnet?

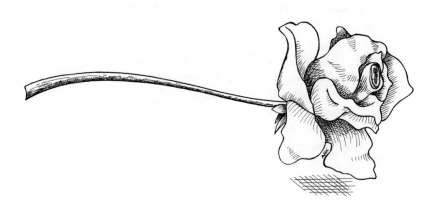

THE WAY IS BEST

Cast not the die, the way is West.
    For a pal and thy that way is best.
Resort not to chance, the life to lead,
    for it's song and dance, so mad indeed.

Oh, shackle thy cares, forget thy mind.
    Peddle thy wares, but be not unkind.
Cast not the die, t'is an ill omen,
    your path is nigh, farewell and amen.

JANUARY 28th, '86

Millions watched the fatal demise
as *Challenger* exploded before their eyes.
What could have been in the minds of the seven
in that dreadful instant of complete oblivion
as we watched the fiery disintegration
reducing to fragments a pride of our nation.

On January 28th, "What went wrong?"
Why did five men and two women die
as astronauts in the Florida sky?
We hang our heads in obvious shame
hopelessly look for someone to blame.
"What went wrong?"

AN OLD MAN'S THOUGHTS

Flakes, white and cold, fell to the earth
  and covered the grass each one to another,
    soon to become a blanket of snow.
      The old man looked at me long.
        "It is snowing," he said.

His words were more than just words,
  They echoed an epoch of a life well spent.
    His eyes deepened the glory of it all
      and gave promise of more to come.
        "Yes, it is snowing,"I said.

Then it came to me, the old man was tired
  of life and age passing him by.
    His thoughts took words, "I no longer cry
      that winter is cold and summer dry."
        "These are child's thought's," he said,
          "and not for such as I."

THE MAID OF GOLD

Troubadors of old have seldom told
the story of *The Maid Of Gold*.
From embattled towers in armor red,
the chatteled flowers in tattle did.

The age-old castle long ago fled,
master and serf these long years dead.
have never heard this charming tale
of *The Maid Of Gold* in this very dale.

The crumbling walls with all their might
I visited one moonless night.
Through portals arched I walked alone
into courts and halls of lifelike stone,

A spiralling stair wound up to the sky,
a rotting chair caught my eye.
I nestled in a niche neath the wall
and faintly heard a far-off call.

I listened well and heard my name,
a voice did speak from the wall aflame.
Hark to my trill and be quite bold,
this, the House of Mall and *The Maid of Gold*.

Prince Mall himself this castle did build
from the blood of all the foes he killed.
He reigned upon this countryside.
Upon this heath he met his bride.

A fair young damsel of hair like corn,
across this moat the Prince had borne.
She ruled his house with iron hand,
yet was loved by all the land.

From balcony above, she sang at night
showered by the moon in golden light.
All were happy in their vast domain,
until drums did roll from men of Spain.

Prince Mall, himself led the charge
and valiantly fought the enemy large.
When day did break the Prince lay dead.
The men of Spain had forged ahead.

All was quiet in the morning cold.
Across the Prince's body lay *The Maid of Gold*.
From her bosom shone a dagger red,
as sun bowed down on her golden head.

The vanquished foe have since departed,
castle walls have crumbling started.
With rack and ruin, wind and rain,
the Prince still rules his proud domain.

Still she sings from the balcony old,
by her Prince, *The Maid Of Gold*.
As the voice died away I searched around,
and a flaming rose by my feet I found.

CHANGES

I miss the pines,
   the sheltering vales.
     grey-brown fields
       and grumbling streams.

I am out to sea
   where it's tides, gales,
     tall white sails
       and oaken beams.

VANISHED LOVE

I love you for what you are
    and not for what you pretend to be.
You may have been a millionaire
    out spending on a spree.

You may have been a pauper
    with this your last big time.
Spending every sou and copper
    with neither reason nor rhyme.

You could have been a lass
    the way that you were dressed.
Your laugh was like a break of glass.
    I'm sure that you were depressed.

You were not known by the crowd,
    of that I am quite sure.
Your face was clouded by a shroud
    of something near demure.

You sat apart and seldom danced
    though invited more than once.
When you did, I caught your glance
    and felt much more like a dunce.

The evening was nearly over
    when I passed by your chair.
I felt my love grow bolder
    as you returned my stare.

I asked if you would share a drink
    of something from the bar.
Your smiled "Yes" made me think
    of exotic spice and shalimar.

We walked along an arched hall
    with scarcely a word to say.
A game of fate without a call
    and not a one to repay.

You nodded over sparkling wine
    when I simply asked your name.
With eager joy I whispered mine
    and waited for your same.

A trumpet blared right near the bar
    your lips kept right in time.
I don't know yet just who you are
    or why your lips met mine.

You faded from within my sight
    you answered not my call.
I seeked you in the dimming light
    and found you not at all.

I'll tell you this, whoever you are
    or wherever you mean to be.
I love you for what you are
    and not for what you pretend to be.

THOUGHTS

Times may change,
    but come what will,
      our thoughts may
        get together still.

For thoughts have learned
    since we last met.
      That hearts that care,
      do not forget.

WE THREE

We knew your name would be Robbie Lou.
    We thought we knew the things you'd do.
We planned your coming right to the day,
    but things just didn't work out that way.

There was a war when you were born
    and from your side your Dad was torn.
When you first saw the light of day
    your Dad was at sea with anchors aweigh.

Your Mommy watched with tender care
    and sent to me your first black hair.
She wrote quite often of your manner
    and prayed to God for my safe return.

In time, I came back safe, to you my son
    and to your Mommy our blessed one.
We laughed, we cried, we felt quite free,
    and I thanked our God for just us three.

GARDEN

I plant the seed
all in a row
because of my need
for it to grow
into a plant
as soon as able
and grant a boon
to grace my table.

PLOWBOY

Let the sweat fall,
    keep the muscles taut.
Forget Springs' call,
    the wind whistles naught.

Yours is to toil,
    to work from dawn to dusk.
With heart in the soil,
    and soul in the dust.

CENTRAL PARK

I see it now, it's all too clear,
    the reason why she called me dear.
You want to know, just who is she.
    Just the girl I thought for me.

Sweet sixteen and pretty too,
    one of God's own chosen few.
Not like all true lovers meet,
    I met her on a busy street.

I caught her eye as she met mine
    and in a flash I knew the sign.
It wasn't long after that when
    I politely nodded and tipped my hat.

She smiled at me so enticingly,
    I knew right then it was up to me.
I couldn't give her, the same old line.
    It must be one she wouldn't decline.

Now, I was wrong, I soon found out,
    she must have thought me a country lout.
She dropped her hankie, or did she throw it,
    right in my path where I would know it.

Returning the token, I asked her name.
    To my dismay, couldn't repeat the same.
We walked along into Central Park,
    dodging the sailors in the dark.

While gazing at the lake so still,
    we decided to stroll up yon grey hill.
Above the lake we found a cabin,
    with same thoughts we both went in.

Then in a corner we did cuddle,
    watching the others in a huddle.
We left the cabin, I bid her adieu,
    not knowing then, my bill-fold too.

This poem was published in the "Arkansas Review" 1944

AN ARCHITECT MAD

This is the story of an architect mad,
who draws the plans of dreams he's had.
Who drinks his Scotch and nips his Rum
and from this source derives such fun.

With pencils and paper, and rulers too,
the things he plans and doesn't do.
Sketches and prints he strews around.
changing a square house into a round.

Erasing a line that must be straight,
making an arch from the figure eight.
With pencil and paper, and rulers too,
he works and slaves, is never through.

Now a cottage small or a palace grand,
could be the work of his artful hand,
but lo and behold the ease and class
to the tipping throat and draining glass.

With pencils and paper, and rulers too,
he begins again with a vigor anew.

BROOKLYN

Shuffled about in a maddened pace,
    I found myself in a wonderful place.
One of the far too many lodgers
    in the home of well-known DODGERS.

I lived in an apartment with my wife
    and shared with her a restful life.
In the two rooms we called our own
    we settled down and made our home.

We spent our hours in different ways
    and in this manner went our days.
Yet, when we went to bed at night
    our neighbors then would start to fight.

Below our window, a cat would call,
    then upstairs a baby would squall.
On the corner, a drunk yelled out,
    then a copper joined the bout.

The guy next door drinking his rum,
    "Let me go. I'll moider da bum."
All over the block radios blare.
    I roll in bed and silently swear.

Night goes on the shades come lower,
    our neighbors' fight is finally over.
Then a barking dog chases the cat.
    A mother screams, "Shut up ya brat."

The weary drunk calls on his feet,
    the copper continues on his beat.
The rum is gone, there is no more,
    the guy next door begins to snore.

Peace approaches within our block,
    morning creeps around the clock.
I fall asleep, to Morpheus I cling.
    With passing time my alarm does ring.

I rub my eyes at this early hour,
    grab my towel and rush to shower.
My coffee is ready when I return.
    The air is crisp with toasty burn.

Breakfast over, I kiss my spouse,
    put on my hat and leave the house.
Now that's a life of strife and sin,
    yet, thank our stars it's genuine.

FORGOTTEN TOY

The rollicking, frolicking toy
no longer a childhood joy,
dusting and rusting as it lay
in attic discard, no light of day.

Begotten, forgotten, a thing of past,
once the pride of a boyish caste.
Aesthetic, cosmetic, no longer thus,
aged in time as one of us.

Disposed, abandoned, with hope shorn.
No tears are shed for this forlorn.
Playful, prayerful there is no sin
for a soldier, with a soul of tin.

WHAT'S VERSE

I tried to write a poem today
and what I wrote in every way
    came to sound as a tick in time
    a game I found as trick in rhyme.
        So I composed from bad to worse
        and as I supposed, I had no verse.

WHAT IS A POET

A poet is:
  a builder of words,
   a gilder of chords,
    a creator of rhymes,
     a recorder of times,
      a teller of tales,
       a seller of veils,
        a mixer of meter,
         a fixer of feature,
          a plotter of schemes,
          a blotter of dreams.

            A poet is one who has
            something to say in a
            non-prosey way.

GRAMPS

Come, stay with me.
A child said to me with a smile,
her dimpled cheek in glee.
On and on, she said, "Just for awhile."
        Gramps stay with me.

Come, play with me.
She pleaded and took my hand in both
of hers, you see.
And softly she whispered to me,
"Just in the sand."
        Gramps, play with me.

GRANDMA'S VISIT

While shopping at the Super Market
I happened to think of the kids.
What would they need?
Milk, bread, cookies and meat
for the sandwiches of course.

Arriving at their home I knew where
to park it, I had been told before.
Don't block the driveway!
Groceries in hand I made for the door,
the sliding door by the wobbly steps.

Upon the steps I balanced wearily,
making for the way to enter.
"Close the door Gram."
My grandson uttered the dire greeting,
"Close the door! You're letting flies in."

REMEMBER SIS!

Remember Sis! Those days ago,
    when we were kids of twelve or so.
    Our country home, high on a hill,
    sheltered from storm, by trees so still.

Remember Sis! Those days of yore,
    honeysuckle vine by the kitchen door.
    Mother's flowers out by the drive
    with roses so red they seemed alive.

Remember Sis! When we were small,
    the sloping lawns, the leaves in fall.
    The narrow lane down to the wood,
    where we would go whenever we could.

Remember Sis! Our High School days,
    we skipped quite often in many ways.
    Your garden of rocks out by the barn,
    Mooch the cat, with a ball of yarn.

Remember Sis! Our plans and dreams,
    dozing in the sun down by the stream.
    Mick and Nell our twin foxhounds
    chasing each other with leaps and bounds.

Remember Sis! The view of the lake,
    a sail on the blue with sparkling wake.
    Picnics and rides out to the falls,
    cool North wind, and wild geese calls.

Remember Sis! The fields and creeks,
    Our happy Dad with all his chicks.
    Daisy, the cow who wouldn't be bossed,
    Lucky our cat who was always lost.

Remember Sis! Those memories old,
    a treasure dear, as good as gold.
    As the years go by, they seldom miss
    a precious past, Remember Sis!

ODE TO "OLD CHARLEY"

We gathered together Alphas to Omegas
    to meet each other in Las Vegas.
It happened at our Poets Convention
    where we cast votes in firm conviction.

To select the very best in verse
    acclaimed by all, with goodly purse.
Poems were read from oats to barley.
    Majority voted the poem "Old Charley."

To me there was something in the thing,
    it somehow possessed a knowing ring.
"It seemed to me I heard that song before,
    it was from an old familiar score."

Some of us talked about this at the time
    and we wondered about a truthful rhyme.
Poetic license gives no one right to steal
    and poetry should come from an inner feel.

It could well be a plagiarism of ideas.
    To a contestant a clear matter of bias.
As Dickens penned, there will be a Marley.
    World Of Poetry will have an "Old Charley."

THE WIDOW'S WALK

So it came to pass, and to score,
the ship *Amanda Lee* was no more.
Word came about, "All hands were lost"
in the Hebredies at one aweful cost.

So she climbs the narrow stair
to a roof-top walk, to look and stare.
Her constant gaze, ever sea-ward
for the mast that must be hers.

She would not cease, in her belief
to accept with an ease, and relief.
He would be back, if not this day,
surely there is to be another day.

Days came and went, one to another.
Friends came in dissent, and no other.
Yet, still she alone, her vigil kept
with wind-strained eyes she sadly wept.

Then came a day, and she did not show.
Those who missed her, did not know.
They buried her with eyes to the sea
and a cut in stone, "Captain And Me."

The house still stands, in a chill,
haunted they say, by a widow still
who looks to the sea in ghostly stalk
as she continues her "Widow's Walk."

SHADOW TALK

Why does my shadow balk,
when it I try to stalk?

I know that it can walk.
Why doesn't shadow talk?

TROUBLES

The perils of misfortune are many,
they cling to me as the cockle-burr
to my dog.

ZODIAC

So, if now and then, I wax sentimental,
don't take my moody facts, detrimental.
For how and when, my act's tempermental,
it depends on Leo's tracts monumental.

PINK ANVIL

With all the strength of years passed by,
you alone have stood the test.
Crumbling walls and wells gone dry
tell the story as would the rest.

The Smithy's gone, the forge long cold,
with shoes and nails and tongs in decay
in an oblivion of aged rust and mould
that mark a part of a yesterday.

There, amidst the rack, ruin and rubble,
you ironically awaited the day
your black iron body would not trouble
to cause anyone obvious dismay.

Found, and removed as an ageless thing,
no longer will your body resound
with steel on steel in hammering ring.
Your soul's to be sold by the pound.

Sold, I see you now in garden of flower
With rocks and frills, and I think,
how could an anvil so dark and dour,
now come to be ever painted pink.

This poem received a Certificate of Merit Award from the World of Poetry

A TOAST

Sailors' lives are soon begotten,
   angry seas and memories last.
      Vanished men are soon forgotten.
         Tilt your throat and drain your glass.

CASUALTY

A hazy mind, a tired eye, a will to live
   and not to die.
A pain that stabs, a body so sore, a brain
   that sees a foreign shore.
A rattle in throat, a prayer on lips,
   a silent curse for devil ships.
A knowing look, a half-sobbed word, sleep
   that wakes in another world.

FREEDOM'S PRICE

Folks all say, it'll be over soon!
Our boys will be home again.
But do they think of rack and ruin,
broken souls, bitter hearts no end?

Where yesterday was a smiling face,
today sees a grim and knowing one.
No antidote can possibly erase
the shock and memory of battles won.

A SPRING

Along the cliff, between the rocks
the bubbling water flows
to form a pool where Nature locks
the gushing spring that grows.

DAYDREAMS

I often think, some day I'll find.
An inspiration to ease my mind.

In visions afar, I would behold
castles of air dipped all in gold,
guarded by high mountains of dew,
painted with colors of varying hue.
Banner of scarlet in breeze do fly
from age-old towers, dizzily high.

The scene will change, my castles vanish
like drifting clouds my thoughts do banish.

SEA GULLS

From on a wall high,
    one and all do fly,
    as the sea gull cry
    in the late Fall sky.

TROPIC SEAS

A moonlit night in the Tropics,
    far out on the rollicking sea.
My sail chock full of frolics,
    now that's the life for me.

THE DOVE

Today, I watched
a Mourning Dove mating.

Or did I watch
a mating dove mourning?

RAINBOW TROUT

The swirling whirling waters carried
the fly on high.
The dancing, prancing feathers, no longer
spry and dry,
came to rest in sullen quest on still-deep
of the pool.

A lightning slash, a white-foamed crash,
a flash of rainbowed jewel,
jarred my wrist with vicious twist as my
rod arched in the plight.
A lashing lunge, a splashing plunge, now
began the fight.

In silvery mist by sunlight kissed, he
leaped the water clean
and froze my heart in every part, my soul
took in the scene.
With sudden spurn, waters churn, my line
cuts through the foam.

Twisting turns and soon he learns, amid
the rocks to roam.
At last subdued, this day I rued, neither
will I forget.
No prouder prize of such a size has ever
missed my net.

This poem achieved a Golden Poet Award of 1987 as well as Certificate of Merit at
the Third Annual Poetry Convention held at Las Vegas, Nevada by WORLD
OF POETRY.

VAGABONDIA

Roam the world, without a care.
    A life awhirl, none shall share.
You're the master, the helm is yours.
    That way is faster, so why shed tears.

Trot the globe, fight the bore,
    in China robe on foreign shore.
Seek for gold, search the coast.
    In heat or cold, make the most.

Comb the beach, in wind or rain,
    clear the breach, once and again.
Stick to your guns when you're due
    and trouble runs, you'll never rue.

Sail the seas, some seven in all,
    mind the ease, of a gypsy call.
In every port, you'll have a time,
    for life is short, without a rhyme.

Roam the world, for it's a curse,
    with a twirl that could be worse.
It's in the blood and so amen,
    if it could, it would never end.

ACID RAIN

Dark clouds so moisture laden
marked with deadly droplets,
drifted, directed by whim of wind
across an impatient nation
with no solution to pollution
and another beclouded lake absorbs
the yellow shrouded rain that falls
and in turn dies in silent wake
only to arise as way of progress.

POLLUTION

We were given a world in natural state.
Our flag unfurled we opened our gate.
A nation of races, this was our aim,
ruination by paces has been our shame.

They say we're free, we've nothing to fear,
the blind cannot see, the deaf can not hear.
Yet all can feel the impending doom
with turn of a wheel and weave of a loom.

In eager fever we've peopled our land
as a gay deceiver with foresight bland.
We've reaped the sea and raped the soil
with destruction to see for all our toil.

We've spoiled our world from sea to tree.
Our air is awhirl with an unpleasantry.
In name of progress we've ignored pollution
and still we continue with no solution.

SEA SONG

I see the sea, it is there,
the wind, the waves, the shore.
Jagged rocks and sea-cliff tops
and gulls that sing and soar.

I hear the sea, it is there,
the swish, the swash, the roar,
washing waves in wind-swept caves
and sands that sing and snore.

I feel the sea, it is there,
the salt, the spray, the foam.
Rocking roll, storm-tossed soul
and a ship that heads for home.

SEAFARER

It's a salty ballad from Panama to Nome,
A sailor has a lady wherever he may roam,
These faces vanish as the sun afore mist,
When anchor is hoisted, put down to rest.

NATURE'S GIFT

To me by far a most beautiful sight,
    a tree covered hill wrapped all in white.
The quiet of the valley below,
    an equal to any that God can show.

The sinking sun brings quiet here,
    and life below, they do not fear.
I am their friend, they know me well,
    not as one who makes life Hell.

They love and trust me, one and all,
    I've often answered their cry or call.
When cold is bitter and wind so high,
    they come to seek me so timid and shy.

Tracks in the snow, small, some huge,
    all seem to lead to my humble refuge.
A haze of smoke in spiral so straight,
    brings to their mind an age-old trait.

Like a flash they go, soon to return,
    for I am their friend, they did learn.
Now it's all for you as well as me
    and it will be so for eternity.

Lose yourself on a starlit night.
    Go find the beauties that you might.
Then thank the God in the wilderness,
    you've seen His world in its tenderness.

RAIN

They say it rained today.
Surely they must be right,
for the air is cleaned away
and heat has left the night.

I should have gone for a walk,
and left my cares behind.
Instead I heard someone talk
on how to live when blind.

WEATHERMAN

The forecast you said would be snow,
reaching depth of five inches or so.
And you said, of the wind of course,
it would reach the fifty mile force.

It came on us in still of the night
from the north with all its' might,
and cowed us with such fury untold,
leaving us all so very, very, cold.

You must have sensed the asininity,
and rapidly you left, our vicinity.
The winds that blew in from Canada,
you somehow missed down in Florida.

We must have known, we had warning,
yet we faced that chilling morning.
But . . . there are things, other than,
taking the word of your weatherman.

URINATION OF MAN

Our streams run yellow with deadly solution
filling and killing life within.
Our lakes become shallow with vile pollution,
a heritage to kith and kin.

Our shores are bespoiled with gaseous oil
so lethal to man, fish and fowl.
Odd spores give birth to a noxious soil,
no longer virile, now foul.

Our land is enclouded with a sinister smog
threatening all that breathe.
Our crops are sprayed with infectious fog
and so suddenly we grieve.

Our trees die out in short time of instance,
no seeds will they now scatter.
Our food may contain some toxic substance
they tell us does not matter.

We are all to blame for we insist on progress
with scarce a thought as to how.
And each does claim we must desist or digress
and the time to do it is now.

Speak out then, with an objection that seethes
in righteous ire and demand
to clean up this world for as everyone sees,
you are a nation of man.

RAINBOWS

One can wonder
and so we ponder,
about the reason why;
Rainbow's in the sky.

Colors red, white, blue
prisms reflecting dew,
deflecting in arched way
to please us as it may.

At the end, a pot of gold
from cradle we've been told.
Yet, never, a person's found
any hint of gold, ever sound.

But with every bow
comes a ray of hope
for calmer days allowed,
promised in each cloud.

We should not wonder,
but in truth sincere,
accept the reasons why;
Our Rainbow's in the sky.

WOODS IN SPRING

The quiet of the woods in Spring,
    does to my heart such solace bring.
I'll wander through glades wet with dew,
    my feet leave tracks where I came through.

Gushing streams put on a show,
    with the help of the melting snow.
Rising vapors from the lake ascend,
    tinging low clouds with frosty blend.

The Mayflower peeps her head through snow,
    the first to come, the first to go.
The woods are filled with a heavenly scent,
    awakened Nature is skyward bent.

From the thicket king pheasant crows,
    to his mate down in the rows.
Deep in the woods a squirrel chatters,
    lending his voice to local matters.

From his post on dead pine so tall,
    sentinel crow bursts forth a call
As he watches my bold approach,
    he warns again not to encroach.

Leaving his post to sky he does soar,
    joined by comrades so many more.
Beneath my feet a grouse flies free,
    knowing not the scare he gave me.

This be mine, my everything,
    the quiet of the woods in Spring.

LEAVES

"Color me red," the leaves said,
and frost was quick to reply,
"your green is dead, so blush ahead
and take wing to the sky."

MY EVERGREEN TREE

It came to me that I've never seen
what to me, is a brown, brown evergreen.
It's not merely one of natures' antics,
nor is it a problem of pure semantics.

The green tree is brown and rightly so
and so it appears against the new snow.
How now, brown tree that should be green,
what has happened, what have I not seen?

Has the North Wind been cruel, biting deep
or the sleet and ice disturbed your sleep?
Is it that you have aged beyond your time
or beguiled, you reconciled to the rhyme?

I do not know why your color is lost,
It must have been at a dreadful cost.
I only know that you are brown to me
yet, ever, ever, my evergreen tree.

WINTER

Flake to flake, one to another
forming a vision of white
with shadowy drifts
tinted bright
by sun.

Cloud to cloud, grey, blue, white
tying sky and tree to earth
with light and dark
mixed with mirth
by wind.

Gusts and gusts, strong, north
bending twig twisting twice
sculpting as she goes
wedded with ice
by cold.

SNOWFALL

Fleecy flakes so soft and faint
strive to paint and decorate
the lonely pine in silent fur
guarding the wood so calm and still.
Life is there, yet none dare stir
for snow descends from yon grey hill.

RELIGION

What does it take to find religion?
    How does one make a final decision?
Some of us find we can't go it alone,
    and like the blind we try to atone.

For we know the power and we do pray.
    Not that we cower, with feet of clay.
So we have spurned our each disaster,
    for we have learned, He's the Master.

We go through life, with guiding hand,
    and so we view strife with no demand.
Yet some will laugh and thus ridicule
    He with the staff and the Golden Rule.

Is it then only, when the end is near
    they are so lonely, and feel the fear?
As death gives nod to move right in,
    they look to God and find religion.

A PRAYER

Oh my God.
　　Let me walk in prayer tonight.
　　Only you can spare the hurt within me.
　　Let me talk that I might be right,
　　by asking for this boon of thee.

Oh my God.
　　I know that I have often strayed
　　from the path that I should follow.
　　Yet, you were with me as I prayed
　　and guided me through this slough.

Oh my God.
　　Why must it be that we feel the need
　　when we are faced with disaster?
　　Is it a way of fate, already decreed
　　for one and all by our Master?

Oh my God.
　　Let me walk in prayer tonight.
　　Grant me power that I could ease
　　all the hurt that you and I might.
　　Be with me Lord, I ask you please.

THE STORM

Darkening sky, off to the North.
  Lightning nigh, in bringing forth
    a promise vow of distant thunder
      in persistent show of storm awonder.

Catspaws dismissed, in silent sway,
  whirligigs assist in stinging spray
    as shift in wind an instant gave
      drift to ascend in constant wave.

One to another, to form a crest
  as in hauteur with all the rest.
    Rain arrives with a noisy beat
      as it strives to equal the feat.

Thunder echoes, across the sound,
  voicing in prose, here and beyond.
    Gusting wind singing the fray
      whistling within, having its say.

Sounds diminish in dying sighs
  sung to a finish on clearing skies.
    Misting rain seeking to uncover
      silent reign, the storm is over.

STINKERS

Three little skunks
  out for a stroll,
    one by one
      in a row.

Little tails upright
  in time weaving,
    one by one
      two and fro.

Three little scents
  a trail leaving,
    phew by phew
      as they go.

BERRY

My name is Berry,
  my kin are many,
    and being oldest,
      am I Elder Berry?

SKOAL

Who can tell the reason why
there's fun in rum and a Martini's dry.
What can anyone possibly do
to botch a scotch or ruin Mountain Dew.

Ours is not to reason why
there's sin in Gin and Canadian Rye.
And why does one truly pine
for Belgian Beer and end with a Wine.

THIRD DECK PHANTASMAGORIA

You lie in your bunk, and look at your feet,
You admit you're sunk, so this is defeat.

You fall asleep, some pass out,
in sweat so deep, it's all about.
The angels depart they fear to tread,
without a chart, near such a bed.

Demons and devils take over your dreams
with antics and revels, jeers and screams.

Next watch goes on, you awake with a dash,
Yes, awake, shove off, douse that flash.
Your clothes you don, on watch you go,
relieve your man and grab your jo.

It's hot as Hell, but it's still your job.
So, it's just as well, for you're only a gob.

This poem was published in "Our Navy Magazine" 1942

SPY EYES

There were demons in her eyes
her glance, a knowing look.

Only then, did I realize.
She read me like a book.

WOMAN

I thought of many things to say
and many things to do.
Yet all in all, in every way
my plans were made by you.

FUTILITY

I know of love, aware of hate
and all the shades between,
and I was born, by way of fate
not a pauper, prince nor queen.

I know of life, fear not death.
I've faced each in its turn.
Tell me Solomon, Saul or Seth,
why love. hate, freeze or burn?

PIER THIRTEEN

A girl, a boy, a moonlit night,
    charming couple, a beautiful sight.
A movie, a soda, and then for a walk.
    Politics and war mixed with the talk.

A lad, a lass, with nothing in mind,
    step with step, a haven to find.
A hint, a look, then off to the pier.
    Hand in hand, they've nothing to fear.

A kid, a Miss, leaning on a rail
    with eyes astare at moon so pale.
A glance, a nod, lost in embrace,
    cheek to cheek, their pulse arace.

A guy, a gal, adrift in a dream,
    across the bay in moonlight beam.
A pretty picture, as in the song,
    but fade away as clock does bong.

A girl, a boy, on pier thirteen.
    Happy youth as we have so seen.
One last kiss, a muffled sigh,
    a fond farewell and so good bye.

TO A BABY BLUE RIBBON
ON A BLUE EYED BLONDE

You're just a baby blue ribbon
on a blue eyed blonde.
You caught my eye, you made me stare,
so listen here and have a care.
Neatly tied you snatched my glance,
hinted to me signs of romance.

Now you were right, oh, did you know?
I fell in love, you so and so.
You bobbed along among the crowd,
brightened my life, lifted a shroud.
You stole my heart, you little thief.
I knew you then in a moment brief.

Hand in hand, you worked with Cupid.
Don't say you didn't, I know you did.
He shot the arrow, you tied the knot.
Neat work my friend, a clever shot.

You're just a baby blue ribbon
on a blue eyed blonde.
Scented so sweet with charming lure,
you knew your job, you got me sure.
Aren't you proud, you baby blue silk.
Candy from a baby, or is it milk.

You're off your throne, yes, in my power,
safe at last from wind and shower.
Between the pages, you'll lie in rest.
Which for you I think is the best.
Your color will fade, but victory is won.
You've had your day and your fun.

Some later day, you'll catch my eye,
make me think, make me sigh.
Good luck old chap, you're still my pet,
without your help, we'd never have met.

This poem was published in the "Arkansas Review"

THE PURPLE HEART

He was waiting for a streetcar, as most folks often do,
leaning against a lamp post and dressed in the Navy Blue.
His face was very thoughtful beneath the small white hat.
His eyes were keen yet, vengeful, I saw from where I sat.

He was more than just a sailor, as one could plainly see,
by the very ease and manner, of this traveller of the sea.
Various colored ribbons were arranged upon his breast,
a record of his battles lodged right upon his chest.

He had already been in the fracas afore the mess at Pearl
in the North Atlantic with his battle colors furled.
He saw some rugged duty on the frigid Eastern Coast
Good conduct did he muster as one did vainly boast.

He was in the South Pacific as one bar plainly told
and action there aplenty by stars thereon threefold.
But the bar that caught my eye, was set quite apart.
He served his country well, he wore the Purple Heart.

PARODY

In a cabin, in a cabin
  on the tin-can one forty-nine,
    stood the skipper, Capt. Dripper
    and his aide with a whine.

Now, Mr. Captain, Mr. Captain.
  We're underway at quarter to nine.
    We've no crew sir, all ashore sir,
      and they're drunk on Italian wine.

Drunken sailors, drunken sailors,
  from the good ship one forty-nine,
    are on the beach Sir, on the beach Sir,
      and they're having a Hell of a time.

Liberty's up, Sir, Liberty's up, Sir,
  and the crew are still ashore,
    and they'll stay there, stay there,
      till the wine, there is no more.

TO THE ENEMY YOUTH

While cannons roar and bombs do fall.
Dictators scream and Emperors do call
for the early youth of the fatherland
with waving banner and marching band.

Their people starve and cry for aid,
while the leaders sit in sodden parade.
Their lads are sent to distant isles
with faces grim where should be smiles.

The bursting bombs forever erase,
the youthful look from every face.
They are men and men should fight
for all their lords think as right.

A sudden burst from some hidden nest
may quickly cease this endless quest.
A bayonet charge in the dead of morn,
the taste of steel and a hero is born.

Screaming shells that land so near
arouse in each heart a silent fear.
A painful cry in a shelter asunder,
your comrade dies with eyes awonder.

Is this your birth, your hearts desire,
to kill and maim with fervent fire?
Where are the carefree, happy days,
the laughing women, the peaceful bays?

The joking throngs, the crowded taverns,
the joyful voices in echoing caverns?
All are banished by the leader's order
and suspicion reigns within your border.

Your mad-man's schemes are all in vain,
for happiness lies in freedom's reign.

GUNS

Some of the people crying out,
    proposing a ban on all our guns.
Remove them they angrily shout.
    Take them we must, from our sons.

Two factions do suddenly emerge,
    those that want and the do-nots,
Each aloud with verbiage urge
    to opinionate the people with Not.

"Guns kill people, take them away."
    End this for all, this missile age.
"People kill people," others do say.
    "We want our guns forever to stay."

Now, who is right and who is wrong
    and who takes part in exhibition?
It was we who fight and we the strong
    who faced a like issue in Prohibition.

THE MORN ATTACK

All hands alert in the morning hours,
watching for planes we know aren't ours.
A droning sound in the distant sky,
a few dark specks ever so high.

The warning alarm with sound so clear
brings crews to their guns nary a fear.
A flight appears from out of the sun
and off the planes peel, one by one.

The barking rifles, the chattering guns,
our boys give Hell to the Imperial Sons.
A shrapnel burst rips a plane asunder,
as bombs near miss causes a thunder.

The smoking tail of a careening plane,
the sight of another all aflame
spur our gunners to carry through
and give the enemy all their due.

The strafing slugs rip up our deck,
our helmsman misses a nearby wreck.
With a final burst the attack is over.
Of diving planes, there are no more.

Now, we look around without a sound,
just to check on who is around.
With a silent prayer our heads do bow,
and we carry on with a muttered vow.

WE HAVE BEEN TOLD

To live by the pen is not enough,
man must look to the sword.
In this life of scuff and rebuff,
fine words shall be ignored.
Bread of life is found in books,
but tasteless is the find.
Man has found in others' looks;
"FIGHT" or be left behind.

Man has learned since days of cave,
that knowledge can be shared.
With painted scene, word and wave,
a better life can be fared.
With food scarce, hunger looked around
and found in man a bitter wretch
who beat his fellow to the ground,
and added to the wall another sketch.

There was He who gave us script
of right and wrong, and good or bad,
we learned from manger to crypt
of the good life that can be had.
"Turn thou the other cheek," He said.
We were again beaten to the ground.
"Drive the changers from the temple."
Our action proved to be sound.

We built towers that crumbled, tumbled,
and heard not each others word.
In great crowds we humbled, grumbled,
Then from the script we heard,
"An eye for an eye, a tooth for a tooth."
In truth we were not a bit dismayed.
For word for word and truth for truth,
thus with life we played.

Man and man, nation and nation,
we fought for our right and wrong.
Clashed and crashed for salvation
and our belief in word and song.
To live by the pen is not enough,
man must look to the sword,
to keep the word, and make it rough
on those who would rule this world.

"RETREAT"

I awoke this morning to say,
"Good Morning Lord,
what have you for me today?"

No more awake and mourning,
"Good God, its morning!"
Somehow He takes all in hand
and willingly "Makes My Day."

No promises of great expectations,
no thesis of creations.
Just another day for us to face,
with His help all falls in place.

This much, in Retreat, I did learn,
to be discreet when fingers burn.
In all dissertation, lesson to be had
with some consideration, good or bad.

So I awake in morning, I learn to say,
"Good Morning Lord,
what have you for me today?"

"Surprise me, Lord."

VICTORY CRY

While conquerors of nations sit,
and view the ill-gotten gains.
Forgotten men with eyes alit,
still live though despot reigns.

Bomb-struck towns in silent night
are wide awake with rebels' feet.
Secret havens still shelter might,
underground there is no defeat.

"V" for Victory, a haunting cry
the vanquished flay invaders pride.
Speechless men, pray for release,
arrests and hangings never cease.

Hungry fighters under flaming skies
hurry for dens in which to hide.
Marching feet of the arm of law
warn the rebels of what's in store.

Grim watchers in wrathful awe, sore,
see their friends in bloody gore,
and their fight goes on and on.

OUR RADIO MARINE

This is a story of a Georgia lad,
    a southern boy with looks not bad.
Reasons unknown, he left his town,
    joined the Marines, oh so renown.

There was a rumor of a skirt,
    who did the boy a little dirt.
Perhaps it's right, I wouldn't know.
    I don't guess so it could be so.

Months later he joined the Fleet.
    He couldn't march, it was his feet.
Oh, he didn't go, he just was sent.
    With saddened heart he left his tent.

Packed his rifle and bayonet too,
    shouldered his pack, followed through.
His orders read to the *USS ARKANSAS,*
    a ship he knew of, but never saw.

He landed aboard with all his gear,
    saluted the colors without a fear.
An officer asked, "What did he know?"
    With tearful eye uttered "Radio."

With bended head he was sent below,
    dragging rifle and his gear in tow.
Sad he was and with bended back,
    made his way to the Radio Shack.

Through the fog and smoke within,
    he peered and visioned a radioman.
Buzzing phones and sparking keys
    soon put the lad all at ease.

"Reporting for duty. What's my job?"
  "Painting and cleaning, just as a Gob."
He soon got used to the life he led,
  but missed above all his downy bed.

After a hard day at lugging stores,
  dreamed that night of Georgia shores.
It's not so bad, although it's HELL.
  He could have spent the night in a cell.

"I've made my bed and so it's mine,
  but these shoes tomorrow I'll shine."
Saturday again and so inspection
  "I'll try again the same deception."

He got away with it, need say more.
  On with the blues and so ashore.
He doesn't drink of that I'm sure.
  He'll probably go to a "girlie show."

Back on board, and so it goes,
  shift into some working clothes.
Scrub the deck, then shine the brass,
  empty the trash and clean the glass,

This and more, it's a lot of work,
  but from that he'll never shirk.
He signs his payslip smile a honey.
  He did his share to earn that money.

You ask me, "What's his share?"
  Take it easy and have some care.
Not what he's done, but what he did
  that makes us like this lanky kid.

So, to the compartment he did go,
  to clean the place, make it show.
In the morning you'll see his face,
  at all this work with steady pace.

He made a name in the Radio Gang,
 for making coffee with a tang.
Oh, it took some time to get that way
 for well do I remember the cursed day.

He made our coffee with salt-water,
 which nearly resulted in a slaughter.
Though we forgave and we forgot,
 seldom ever would he touch the pot.

Up at dawn he fell into muster,
 with dirty rifle and all afluster.
With solemn face, he stood his ground
 and watch the Sarg make his round.

An angel must take care of him
 to get away with such a sin.
Through the pace of the daily grind,
 he was always a step or two behind.

And when it came to The Manual of Arms,
 he resembled a kid fresh from the farms.
He got away with the lot you know,
 but remember this he's in "RADIO."

Such it is, but it is an excuse,
 so ragged and worn with much misuse.
Yet the lad did know his stuff,
 in his work he would never bluff.

Knew his books, could snow one under
 with watts and ohms, sounds athunder,
He studied his course and made a rate,
 the angel again, how kind was fate.

Now he sits with phones on head
 with staring eyes and feeling dead.
Watch on watch, from morning to night.
 Gosh, but don't he look the sight.

And in the day you'll find him sunk
   out of sight within his bunk.
Wakening hours you'll hear him sing.
   It is then your ears start to ring.

This isn't all, there's more to come,
   my little tale is not yet done.
The lad so tall and yet so sad
   has yet to do something really bad.

Away in Culebra, Panama and Ponce,
   his line the same, he did not dance,
Yet with the Janes he made a hit.
   In every port he did his little bit.

Now each, every time he met a skirt,
   she did her best to get his shirt.
He's wise to the tricks, to the game.
   He seldom troubles with the same.

Then came the cruise with the Middies
   running the ship like little kiddies.
T'was on this cruise he became a fan
   of ole man "Sol" for he got a tan.

Such as it was, he claimed it so
   but as I said, "I wouldn't know."
An accident occurred, it was a trifle,
   our gallant Marine had lost his rifle.

He lost it on the deck, he did reckon,
   and found it with some Seaman Second.
His time is short, he'll head for shore,
   and for the sea t'will be no more.

He dreamed last night, fields of clover,
   swears to God, he'll never ship over.
Now that's his story, we have ours.
   We really believe he'll miss us Tars.

Drawing plans of the house he'll build,
    soon he'll join the Homemakers Guild.
Things he's done, will fill these pages,
    but to tell and retell would take ages.

So, I'm going to end this satire
    and to my bunk I shall retire.
But before I end this tale of woe
    remember this wherever you go.

If you see this Marine on land,
    step right up and shake his hand.
He's done his part his worries o'er
    he kept his word he never shipped over.

NOTE: This is the somewhat true story of a Marine from Georgia who shipped out on the *USS ARKANSAS* as a Radio Operator. His name I think should be kept from this sheet reasons that are obvious. Any of the personnel in the Radio Gang from September 22, 1939 to September 10, 1940 can vouch for the authenticity of this little tale. Lou Fendrick.

WANDERLUST

The time has come, so go he must.
    Under his feet there gathers no dust.
A tramp to some, a vagabond to others.
    To me, one of God's own nature lovers.

Worries are few though the roads are long.
    He's on his way, heart full of song.
Walk or ride, it's all up to fate.
    Who gives a damn whether he's late.

SALVATION

From atop my oil-drum pulpit,
I reveal to you many things.
Dreams and screams of young
and reams of schemes untold.
I am your preacher recall.
So off your stumps
and kneel you all.
Sinners you be,
salvation is
mine.

LOOK HOMEWARD ANGEL

Look homeward angel
for can't you see?

Those words you heard
that had you scared
were not from me.
Be not deceived
by what they see.

It was never so and
never will it be
for you and for me
there's an eternity.

Look homeward angel
and be with me!

ARETHUSA FROSH

They hail from sky blue waters,
from hills so far and near.
They are the fondest daughters
of those they love so dear.

They are the girls of Normal,
they are the Frosh of today.
Not too harsh, not too formal
fresh and sweet and always gay.

They greet you with a smile,
they invite you in to stay,
and make it worth your while
to find the Arethusa way.

They treat you like a brother
and seldom pass the chance
to have you meet their Mother
and then go out to dance.

Their welcomes are becoming,
their farewells, quite demure.
To Arethusa you'll be coming,
of that I am quite sure.

They hail from sky blue waters,
from hills so far and near.
They are the loyal martyrs
who've learned to know no fear.

MY LOVE

There isn't a day go by
when I don't think of you.
There isn't a way to say
my love for you is true.
You see, you're the one for me
and will be so for eternity.
So don't ever let a day go by
without your not knowing why.

ENGAGED

It is not a matter of consequence,
this knot of patter of coming events.
Tell me dear, do you really believe.
Is your mind quite clear, not deceived?
Are you truly in love, or only foresee,
    a life of ease, and security?

DEVOTION

The awareness of you is meaningless
    without your devotion so true.
Yet, this must do, I will confess
    until aware of me, too.

MERCY

He felt her pulse with practiced hand
that knew the end was near.
Biting pangs of agony took her breath away
and she looked at him, pleading for a way
to end her suffering, cease her pain that
would not be denied, deep, deep inside.

He shook his head and felt the tremor
of approaching death thru his fingers
and into his very heart affecting them both.
Yet, he remembered his oath, a sacred trust
all who practice must abide.

He never questioned his action as he slowly
reached within the bag along his side.
Swift and sure, needle pierced the skin.
She relaxed, eased and smiled gratefully
for she did not feel the clean sharp break
as the steel slowly deadened the pain.

She was dead, so her smile said
and carefully he drew the sheet, wondering
in an off hand manner.
Had she really died or did he truly murder.

MEMORIES

Right now I miss,
a fishing trip, the grey brown streams.
The open fields and the promising dreams.
My little old dog, she's Black and Tan.
Flapjacks on the fire, coffee from a can.

Oh how I miss,
my smelly coat with loops for shells.
A battered old hat, my hunting compels.
My trusty gun with barrel so true
the outline of birds against the blue.

I'll always miss,
those shaded woods, with scent of pine.
The valley below, I think of as mine.
The call of the geese on wing so high.
The rising sun on the tinted sky

Right now I miss,
the falling leaves, the call of the wild.
The freezing nights with days so mild.
The open fire at the end of the day,
and drinks to success, no more to say.

THE LONELY GOOSE

From the back waters of Hudson Bay
to the slack waters down Cajun way,
one finds family called Anserinaes,
a term known only to Canadian Geese.

Trumpet-toned calls echo the skies.
Each fall in line following a wise
gander who seems to have his say,
for from here to there, knowing the way.

Strange as it seems, geese have no strife
because once mated, they are wed for life.
Not like man we know, geese are monogamous,
despite their often discordant, cacophonus.

During the gunning season, late in fall,
one often hears the single lonely call.
Circling the skies, he seeks too late,
not knowing shell-shot killed his mate.

So when you hear that mournful sound,
when you see him search the ground,
in your mind you will come to reason,
why did God create this gunning season.

Yet, each year coming, Spring or Fall,
we eagerly await their mating call
migrating geese so high in the sky
we welcome them back with a sigh.

Our lonely one rejoins the flock and
in plaintive voice can only mock the
others in determined flight assign, for
you see, he's the only one out of line.

CHILDHOOD DAYS

I wandered today in my slumbering thoughts
    to my childhood days, my boyhood haunts,
I walked through woods near my home
    and waded the creeks where I did roam.

I found myself on the lighthouse pier
    and hailed the boats as they stayed clear.
I called my dog with a whistle shriek
    and laughed aloud at his face so meek.

I climbed through trees filled with cherries
    and rubbed my face red from the berries.
I fought again with the kid on the block
    and painfully felt that terrible sock.

I swung on the vine at the swimming hole
    and triumphantly yelled in Tarzan role.
I broke a window with my new air gun
    and showed my pals how fast I could run.

I wondered today in my awakening haze,
    if youth today have such wonderful days.

SOLITUDE

In the dimming dusk of a darkened day,
I entered a weird wood.

My martyred mind. I knew did find a way
as it surely should.

PEACE

A tranquility of mind.
Each to each, one to another.

Peace

restfulness of a kind,
man to man, nation to nation.

Peace

a word that has not died,
all in all, not to be denied.

A World of Poetry peace offering August 11, 1987 in Las Vegas 3rd Annual Poetry
Convention

NONE BUT THE LONELY

Am I my brother's keeper?
    Am I our mother's weeper?
Is it why we scarcely care,
    do or die, we barely aware.

We are homeless on the street
    where we roam less in defeat.
Steaming grate our nite abode,
    demeaning fate but out of cold.

Breakfast in morn out of a can,
    the look forlorn seen by man.
Curse you not this way of a city.
    It's all we've got, more the pity.

Dispel the frown, we are outcasts.
    You see us in town as downcasts.
In street we dwell and so we cope
    to exist as well, in forever hope.

That this is wrong, we must agree.
    Yet, will is strong, but can I see.
This is not living, this way of life,
    yet we are giving a cause for strife.

Morning to night our life progress,
    where ever we might our way digress.
Can it be, you and I are the only
    who can see, "None but the Lonely."

RENEWAL

Please return this form with your check.
    "You've already paid?" Then what the heck.
You can't blame us, for we have reviewed
    and find it fact that you've not renewed.

We desire you with us for another year,
    so kindly remit and please let us hear.
We've much to offer, beyond description,
    May we continue with your subscription?

YOUR BUCKS' WORTH

It is true that we make a buck today,
    but about its worth, I'll have my say.
Somehow it does not make much sense
    when that buck has lost its cents.

One thing that may really vex us
    is what we pay in all our taxes.
We pay and we pray that all can live
    and from day to day we continue to give.

In this age of our forever giving,
    I'm in a rage at our cost of living.
Why worry about State Of Nation
    when we can't stop growing inflation.

NO MORE TUNA

There's no more Tuna
in Altoona, tonight.
We have Shad and Scrod,
Mussels and Clams,
and for the Hell of it
a better buy on Halibut.
Lobster, shrimp are choice.
We wait to hear your voice.
But, Yes, we have no Tuna
There's no more Tuna
in Altoona, tonight.

NO TV

The wind came in from the North
on that early December morn.
I heard the sound, half-awake
turned around for my self sake.
Somehow I returned to a slumber
only to arise to a task encumber.
The noise I heard was my antenna
crashing down away from Heaven.
Now this was bad, as bad can be,
That's why I'm mad, mad with no TV.

MAN

And so the world was made,
and He who created,
looked upon his work and sighed.
Then he made man.

What is man?
Man, a creature created by Him,
male or female, no whimsy, no whim
can decide, yet we abide.

Man is a brain, walk, but first crawl,
logic and sane, talk but first bawl.
Man is a being and so being,
man is man.

"Live with the world," He said.
It is yours."
And man lived and loved, in the
world and with the world.

But man being man,
lived not wisely, and lost the word,
"Live with the world."
Son and daughter lived and loved.

Greed, malice, hunger, looked at man
and laughed. "We are a part of man,"
they said, and went to work
to fight, maim and to kill.

Wars became more wars and man
could not destroy man fast enough.
Time, the measure incalculable
blended man's day into day.

Grey dawn dimmed on dusty world,
Man was no longer Man.

SMOKE RINGS

It's only a pipe, made of briar,
    filled with tobacco all afire.
Joy and content it does bring,
    when my troubles start to sing.

LION'S SHARE

Why do they call the lion, King?
Is he not most noble of beasts?
His roar belies with lying ring
at the kill in which he feasts.

Provided as devined by lioness,
who really looks worse for wear.
Come now, Royal One, do confess,
are you entitled to lions' share?

FINI

To destroy one's thought
    you annoy for naught.
As anyone can plainly see,
    what's done is fini for me.

A POET'S WORD

They know how well I miscalculate,
thus tongue-in-cheek, I prevaricate.
Knowing well that I must masticate
each glowing word that I predicate.

SO

When it is so confusing
to find life so abusing.
I find it quite amusing
it's me you're accusing.

SCRATCH

Scratch where it itches,
waste not a single act.
Reap you well, the riches
coming from this very fact.

DANCE

In a delicate distinction
called nuance,
I find discernment
in a new dance.
Yet, movement
so nouveau
won't go.

THE IRS BLUES

April fifteen for we that are lax
    is deadline for filing income tax.
For me it is not the best of news,
    it's then I get the old IRS blues.

I figure out to the nearest cents,
    working around my medical expense.
And somehow I feel that seduction,
    when I recheck my lousy deduction.

It's then I am in utter confusion,
    losing my mind in stock exclusion.
And will there be any retribution
    for what I list as a contribution.

You know I haven't felt so sporty,
    since filling in my old ten-forty.
I end the night, somewhat stunned,
    to find I am entitled to a refund.

SCORN

The harshness of biting words
like a parry thrust
cut deep into the scarlet and
a point is scored.

Yet, duel as we might with
words or blades,
there's no sadder plight
than being ignored.

VIOLENCE

Violence give birth to violence,
    and so the pattern goes.
It is no matter of consequence,
    as each one really knows.

Cain slew Abel, brother to brother,
    manslaughter found the day.
Vain grew able, other and another,
    mans' daughter joined the fray.

RUSTY

Tribute to one, ever remain,
Rusty was his name
with no great claim
to sire in canine fame.

As a Golden a deceiver
passing by as a Retriever.
In eager joy he gave his all
to run in fun with a tennis ball.

Nose to ground he would track
a rolling ball away and back.
Then he came to you, ball in jaw,
nudge you with a clawing paw.

"Give me the ball," I would urge,
but never, ever, would it emerge.
Then he would run, his day was made.
You've been in a game he has played.

Years passed by, red turned to gray
but still he had his puppy way.
He loved to wallow in the snow
and lose his ball on the go.

Sometime he just had to roam
to visit friends away from home.
Then came the day he didn't return,
and of his death we did learn.

That was the day, when I did rue.
Rusty was not my dog, true,
but he was my buddy friend
who came to see me, even in the end.

POET'S WORD

Working with words
Roget would say,
"The right word
in the right place."
A poet could say,
The right word
in the write space.

CANDID

Can . . . . . .
a candid can
be candid
if a can did
a Can-can?
A can did!

GREEN

"It is Spring."
the old man said.
"How green
the grass are."

NOMAD

Now:
No man did
as nomad did,
and why did
nomad do
as no-man did?
Now.

A CLUSTER

Bees in business
buzzing to muster
in fervent fire,
and all afluster
in no lacklustre
to form a cluster
in moment so grand
as Stand of Custer.

RIGHT ON

"Right On" you hear today,
and what that means
I really can't say.

Time was when "all was Jake"
and truth to tell
what more could we take?

But surely you do remember,
"Scram" and "21 Skidoo"
died in glowing ember.

In time all pass in review,
each becoming passe,
and "Right On" too.

MIAMI

I'll start right out with an honest rhyme,
thanks to you girls for the swellest time.
You wined us and dined us, all with a style.
You kissed us and missed us with a smile.

We've sailed the seas, some seven in all,
we've roamed the leas, to a distant call.
From Eden to Hades we've chosen our pals,
and now you ladies, are our fondest gals.

A toast to you lass, you're five of a kind,
break your glass, our friendship to bind.
Remember tomorrow, our days of the past
banish your sorrow, go look for our mast.

MARION

The time has come so go she must,
    under her feet there gathers no dust.
You want to know, just who is she?
    One of our best, we call her Bilsky.

We'll do without her, we'll carry on
    without the hustle-bustle of Marion.
It's over forty years she's slaved away,
    hardly ever late and seldom missed a day.

Times were rough and we got an earful
    but most the time she would be cheerful.
And when we could have climbed a wall,
    she helped us get back on the ball.

When pressure's on, our Marion's fine.
    She'll stick to her job in nick of time.
It's a tribute to Gus, her better half
    who waits it out and still can laugh.

Patience aplenty he sits in the dark,
    out in front where his car is parked.
Duke their dog, will sit by his side.
    and in the back seat Marion will ride.

We know you'll miss us, one and all,
    so come and see us, give us a call.
We love you Marion, you're so inspired,
    it's a crying shame that you've retired.

God bless you, Gal. You've done your best,
    so be assured, you've earned your rest.
Best of Luck, Marion a fondest farewell,
    from all of us, here at Ole Ma Bell.

PASSING GLANCE

It was my duty to smile so,
I knew her dear, so long ago.
Do not pout, and don't deny.
I'll let it out, tell you why.
Beauty is where beauty be.
Can you my love, have doubt
of me?

A PHOTOGRAPH

It's just a picture on my locker door
of a girl I did once adore.
Her face brings back memories
so long forgot of yesterdays.

It's been so long since I knew her,
yet, t'was she who called me dear.
Maybe she still thinks of those days
and remembers all my funny ways.

About the time we ran out of gas.
Our little story that did not pass.
Those were the days, yet did we know
our ways would part and away we'd go.

RETIREMENT

Combine the years,
    add them once more.
Confirm the years
    you know the score.

It's just a human quirk
    to really want to work.
So why am I so inspired
    when I know I'm retired.

Don't count the years,
    accept them with grace.
To Hell with your fears
    you've new life to face.

A TWO YEAR OLD

Then I took you to the farm today
    where the snow in drifts was deep.
      For a two year old you got your way
      and climbed the slopes so steep.

I watched your eyes light up with joy
    as you scampered to the top,
      as if you'd found a long lost toy
      and a way to scare your pop.

PROTEST

There is a feeling today of unrest
an uneasy feeling of dire dismay.
Youth and the world seek a quest
and all have something to say.

They have their day in every way
and protest loud and strong
of high-test cloud seeded with decay
and we all know that this is wrong.

The ills of the world are many
as card and word point out.
But is this the way, if any,
you don't kill pain with a shout.

There are those who sense the plight,
and work within their edgy border
to silently strive for the right
to bring our house back to order.

WHO'S TO BLAME

So, I made a mistake;
   And you're not forgiving?
      Well pardon me for living.
         It's more than I can take.

You've never made a boo-boo?
   Did a thing you knew wrong,
      then cover up really strong.
         Say not so, because you do-do.

WHERE THERE'S FIRE

A touch of a lever,
  a flick of flame.
   We're really clever,
    a trick we've tamed.
   Flint and steel
    many years ago
     brought the feel
      and warmth of a glow.
    We have advanced,
     but have we learned
    to be enhanced,
     our finger's burned.